America
Can Live
Happily
Ever
After

Children's
Version

Elizabeth Wiley MA JD, Pomo Elder

Order this book online at www.trafford.com
or email orders@trafford.com

Most Trafford titles are also available at major online book retailers.

Print information available on the last page.

ISBN: 978-1-4907-9350-4 (sc)
ISBN: 978-1-4907-9349-8 (e)

Our mission is to efficiently provide the world's finest, most comprehensive book publishing service, enabling every author to experience
success. To find out how to publish your book, your way, and have it available worldwide, visit us online at www.trafford.com

Any people depicted in stock imagery provided by Getty Images are models,
and such images are being used for illustrative purposes only.
Certain stock imagery © Getty Images.

Trafford rev. 01/25/2019

www.trafford.com

North America & international
toll-free: 1 888 232 4444 (USA & Canada)
fax: 812 355 4082

THANK you to TIM G. WILEY for his allowing us to use the photographs he sent to you as chosen by the lay out department. The pictures are all nature, pets, etc, to inspire our class participants to learn to enjoy and be grateful for all the world gives to us, rather than be limited by material items they do not have, or have found themselves to be dissatisfied with when they have managed to get them.

Once upon a time, anytime, but right now is good, a few hundred million children were born on this earth.

As they opened their little eyes, they saw beautiful hospitals, beautiful fields, and horrible slums.

Even in the slums the children saw clouds sailing by in the sky, and learned to make animal shapes out of the clouds as adults, or other children taught the words to know what the shapes might look like.

Children in expensive pre-schools learned to lay on the sand in the playground and watch clouds go by and make animal shapes out of the clouds and asked their teachers what the animal words were. Some of those children had teachers who brought out their latest smartest phone and showed them pictures of the real animals and told them the names, and where the animals still might be alive.

Dragons and unicorns, Phoenix birds with their long curled tails, and beautiful crowns on their heads, long necks. The phone showed them ALL things of imagination and dreams today, no longer here, except in the hearts of children and teachers who have a heart of a child. The phone showed them the real animals endangered by humans all over the world of being extinct due to pollution, mining and factory farming.

Some of the children went home and tried to tell the adults what they had seen. Rich or poor, some had adults, old, or young, with hearts of a child who helped them learn to make mythical animals come back to life in their own hearts.

Many native nations believe dragons, like wolves, bears, and other big apex predators are important to life. Many native nations believe that it is up to you which dragon (wolf, bear, shark, dinosaur, or whale) in your own imagination and heart you feed. This means that if you feed the good parts of yourself, you will do the things to make our Creator honored and happy, if you do the bad things, you will make our Creator (and usually anyone who loves you, and often yourself unhappy).

At first, most children looked around the world, and some were lucky to have Elders and other children to answer their questions, or even to carry them around and show them wonderful things and tell them the names and stories about those things. Most Native Nations also tell the children the relationships between Creator and humans and the need to keep balance with nature.

Other children were just taught that most of nature was either to make money, or to get rid of so humans could make more money on the land they had destroyed, from the forests they had killed, from the waters they had polluted and the air they had destroyed.

Many children were being taught that every human would perish along with all of nature if we did not clean up the mess left by thousands of years of greedy humans. It was time for all humans to take a part in cleaning up and restoring the earth. It was time to stop fighting and figure it out.

Many children were taught that our Creator was getting tired of our human antics, and it was time for ALL of us to make sure there was an earth, and nature, and balance for those children who were here, and any children to come in seven generations or more. It was time for ALL humans to respect one another and learn to work together, or maybe our Creator was finally going to let us all reap the horror we had sown in centuries of greed and war.

Many native nations have a version of the phoenix, a bird of mythology that when burnt and destroyed rises from the ashes, better than it had been before. The mythical story is to help humans learn to overcome bad things, and rebuild their lives and those lives around them into better lives than those that led to the destruction of the bird. Many of the stories say the phoenix was destroyed by its own greed, others say it was destroyed by the greed of other humans.

Nature builds itself back. God or Creator as we believe is bigger and longer lasting than the problems of humans, but many nations believe that if mankind finally manages through war, pollution, overuse of natural resources, and killing off all the wildlife to end life on earth, life will restore, just without humans.

Each of us must take our joy in the world and give back joy to the world by taking care of it.

The end of this story is up to each one of us.

We can sit and complain and blame, we can sit and suffer and die, blaming others, or we can do what each of us can to make life better, for ourselves, for nature, for those who share this planet, and restore and take care of all, including each other.

The choice belongs to each person.

The choice belongs to each parent.

What is your choice???

What can YOU do????

That is what this book is about.

Look at the pictures, take your phone out and share pictures of how amazing nature and each other are. Respect Elders. Elders, earn the respect of all. There are more good people on this earth than bad ones. As the old saying went "What if THEY gave a war, and nobody came"..

We have courts, we can simply sit down and enjoy the clouds until the world changes. How we ask can that happen? That is what this book is about.

Each of us has the answer for our own life. Which dragon, wolf, bear, whale shark are YOU going to feed?

While this is the end of this story, the rest of this book will help you form your opinion and actions. Each of us has to decide, is this the beginning, or the end…….which dinosaur will you feed?

SHORT STORY,
written by a six year old who lost his Dad
to the draft and VIETNAM WAR.

THE LORDS OF NOTHING

Asking kids to write books about their feelings, and what is in their tiny hearts leads to amazing outpouring, both of knowledge and of experiences most adults would not know how to handle.

One such story was from a six year old, he wrote a kids story about the people of the world becoming tired of the constant war, death, draft and poverty and heartbreak caused by war.

Using a scripture from their Christian Bible some of the children decided to call the project SIPS, or the turning of swords into plowshares mentioned in the Bible. Even children of other religions agreed this was a good name for a project that would in fact turn the huge modern day sword into "plowshares' Not really plow pieces, but into a museum to help people learn to live in peace together on the earth.

This story was sent to the then President, and in reality, there are now several decommissioned Navy boats and aircraft carriers which now are Naval museums whick memorialize all the battles and wars they fought in. Memorialized all who died on those Naval boats, and their support boats, and aircraft.

One of these ships is in the San Diego harbor and open to the public often to let people visit and remind themselves that war is not just waving flags, and shouting for our side, like a football, or baseball game. These big boats are floating cities that have only one reason in life, to protect the shores of the United States of America and its territories.

What, the children asked, were these ships doing in wars for other nations to keep their empire building going.

That is a question every parent must research and answer for themselves and their children.

Another story written by one of the IMAGINE program groups of youngsters was a story about a CIA operative who was being given an assignment to go to a nation in S. America to "terminate" a risk to democracy in that country.

IMAGINE programs were a program in which children and teens were asked to "imagine" what the world might be like if war was to cease, and crimes were to cease without putting half the adults and a third of the juveniles in prison. To be honest, statistics given out over the past four or five years by the CSPAN covered hearing of the reform justice hearings of Congress and the Justice Department and several private think tanks have shown America has more of its citizens, and illegal and legal aliens in prison than any other country in the world. We wrote to Yoko Ono and asked her if she minded if the children and teens used the work "Imagine" although not using the title of John Lennon's most famous song for any financial reason, they wanted to respect her, and ask. She said no problem.

In the story of the CIA operative, the outcome of the story was that the operative got to the nation he was investigating and found the person he was assigned to "terminate" was a Scout leader, who helped churches and community centers learn about America, and Democracy and how people can be free and honor and respect one another. He also found out the person doing the teaching, helping the people to raise funds to do their programs, was in fact himself, not just in that country when he had been there before, but in other nations where he had assignments.

The youths left the story for each reader to figure out for themselves.

What would happen? How did the CONSTITUTION apply???

The youths sent their story to the head of the CIA at that time.

INTRODUCTION

This book is for parents to work with their children to help them grow up happy and remain happy.

The workbook starts below: There are questions to ask your children and to learn yourself more about America and how we ALL can learn to live "Happily ever after" and to spread happily ever after around the world. We can learn to enjoy happily ever after from other cultures as well.

Americans CAN LIVE HAPPILY EVER AFTER was the oritinal workbook for Americans to read, to adjust to their own lives and live up to the life the Founders of this country, the Native Americans who have made peace with the genocide of more than 800 native nations, and the theft of lands that were NOT filled with bunny people waiting for Cortez, Columbus and other terrorists, racists, and genocidal mercenary troops to come and destroy thousands of years of civilization. AND all those who have given money, their lives and their spouses, parents, sons and daughters to wars to protect the rights envisioned as a continuous government OF the PEOPLE, BY the PEOPLE and FOR the PEOPLE.

These past three years of hate and division, while few are looking at the long lasting despair, crime and drug addiction of our youth that are results of what WE as a nation have allowed to become the mess we live in.

IF you are one of the fortunate thousand or two across this nation that both have money to live around the mess, or even one of the fortunate who have only the broken-ness, no dreams, drug addiction of their children then this book is NOT for YOU.

IF you are one of the overpaid, over educated many who sit in conferences with expensive catered meals paid for by the taxpayers, talking about how many books you have read about commas, then this book is NOT for you.

Benjamin Franklin, among others who founded this country had few years of formal education. HOWEVER, Benjamin Franklin DID go and learn from the Native Nations to find out how they had more than 800 nations, from the top of Alaska, to the Southern tip of S. America, and all the islands along all the coasts that lived in peace for centuries. IF one learns about the Native Nations, one finds out that these millions of people had made huge mistakes, and learned from them. War was not working. Using up all the assets of nature was not working, and they had built cultures around laws that helped people get along and make the world BETTER for the next seven generations to come after them.

Many of those who came to America came to get away from what the Natives call the greedy, and the uncivilized.

They learned from the Native Nations that if you cut down ALL the trees, and put the same crops in, over and over and over, it kills the SOIL, and famine results. They learned that if you kill all the animals and sell their hides to traders to sell in the european empire building nations, soon the animals and fish ran out, and once again famine and death resulted.

The history we have learned has been influenced by people who had their families murdered, their stock stolen, the plants animals, and even the water, air and soil destroyed for momentary wealth for a very few.

Today many Americans have realized that if humans abuse each other, the crime, wars, and division lead to fear, maiming and death. Today many Americans have realized if you just throw trash all over, and ruin the lands, water and air, you are going to perish yourself in famine, natural disaster, and divisiveness that harms all humans and nature.

Einstein told us that to do the same thing, over and over, expecting different results was insanity. It has taken four hundred years for the genocidal, racist, nature hating people who came to America to destroy the people, land, nature and even water and air.

It is time for us ALL, starting with the children who have to inherit this nightmare to set about healing ourselves, the earth and nature.

WE CAN LIVE HAPPILY EVER AFTER. But, we are going to have to change our views. One of the most dangerous persons on earth are those who say "what can we do", "that is just how it is", or "we are made to suffer", and other negative excuses for NOT doing anything to change our own lives and make the world a better place for not just ourselves, but for all, and the next seven generations.

FIRST STEP FORWARD

The first step for every human is to look at reality and ask "is this really how I want life to be?"

The richest of people live sad, strained lives, attempting to stay away from criminals, wars, and revolutions that put them in danger.

Many of the richest people are so unhappy in their own lives they use drugs, whether prescription or street drugs, drink to excess, and grieve their families with many other forms of addiction. Sexual, gambling, refusing to grow up, shopping, over eating, starving to look a certain way, even addiction to plastic surgery.

This book is asking, as a first step to help your children grow up happy and live happily ever after, to admit there is a problem. If we fail to admit there is a problem, we will surely fail to overcome that problem.

SECOND STEP FORWARD

In our programs we ask that everyone introduce themselves with this simple sentence: Hello, my name is………and I am wonderful because God created me. Then we ask each person to add something that they are unique and able to do that makes them happy.

We do NOT decide what religions, if any, are THE one. We do however submit the thought of one Rabbi who said, that if a person makes toothpicks, the factory has rooms filled with employees, and filing cabinets and computers filled with the plans and how to make those toothpicks. How then does the Universe run without an Administrator?

This step means to CHOOSE something to teach your children that helps them find the strength and courage to deal with life, the peace of mind to deal with the things each of us finds in life that we can NOT change, and wisdom to know the difference.

These three choices are from all the Twelve Step Programs. There are commercials for drug and addiction programs that say WE are NOT a Twelve Step Program. Many 12 Step programs themselves do NOT follow their own principles. It is up to each one of us, to learn, and to teach our children to choose a life that helps us avoid all the pitfalls humans create for themselves, to live through all the heartbreak and evil other humans put on each other, and to find the wisdom to avoid the bad things, and ENJOY in peace of mind and heart the good things.

Twelve Step programs as well as the many quasi 12 Step programs that exist all teach that no matter what YOUR personal relationship to a Higher Power, God is a must in our lives. For parents, this means finding God and Creator, and helping your children to sidestep much of the life you led, going down the wrong pathways, by NOT having a God and Creator to rely upon, to stand with you, and to serve, love and honor.

PERSONAL RESPONSIBILITY

This is an important part of life to help a child grow to become a resilient and happy, peace-filled, good citizen of this world.

YOU need to learn this to teach it to your children.

YOU may cross a street and get hit by a car. BUT it is YOUR responsibility how you react to that event.

There are many people who have become very disabled, yet they have picked themselves up, and looked for joy in life, and asked, what did I want in life, and moved ahead, no matter what that means in changes to their original plans.

Teach children to OWN their own lives. With JOY and grace.

One woman told me that she had grown up in a really poverty ridden part of Mexico. She later met a man who had gotten a Visa and moved to America and finally gotten his citizenship. He came back for her, and they moved to his home in a nice neighborhood of S. California. She went to city college and got a nice job, and eventually stopped working to care for their children, and home. After the children went off to their own lives, she decided to take a class she had always wanted to take. She said, you know, I never knew how poor we were (they had lived in cardboard nailed over wood her Father had found in the dump, the kids helped their Mother and Grandmothers get water in buckets their Father found at the dump, walking miles to filthy rivers and creek beds. The kids watered the plants, and chickens and helped sell vegetables and fruits they grew at the city farmer's market. They bought material and sewed (by hand, no electricity even if they had been able to buy a sewing machine). Often the material was salvaged from thrown away clothing her Father had found at the dump. Few toys, often just found by their Father at the dump and washed clean by Mother and Grandmother.

Yet, she had never felt sad, or bad, or without. Until she moved to S. California and realized how horribly poverty stricken they had been. Over the years they sent money home, and her Mother and Grandmother were able to build a small house and a small sewing shop, to continue to sell hand crafted items and produce at the city market. They loved their village, and friends; their family was there. Those little old ladies were happy and thankful for all they had been given in life, and that their children and grandchildren wanted them to be happy, whether they came to America, or built a family farm for the next generations to come visit on holidays.

This story made me realize that when we give charity, it is necessary to give with honor and respect to those we "help", otherwise we are just building our ego, by demeaning other people.

This is an important lesson for ALL children and the adults who raise them.

HELP YOUR CHILDREN live with JOY and DREAMS. One day the small daughter of a friend was looking through a mail order catalog and saying "I am going to get this"…and that. Her Mother snarled at her, YOU AINT GOING TO HAVE NOTHING. Told her to throw the booklet away and shut up. I was really upset. YET, when I listened to her, she was very upset over the fact that she had gotten an eviction notice on her home that day, the one her husband's VA payments had gone to, from his severe disabilities from serving in Vietnam. It turned out the realtor who had sold them the home did not own it, he had just been scamming off a rental, and when the owner sold it, the realtor walked away free. The court said the woman had no claim, even though she had papers and fraudulent deeds.

NO WONDER she told her daughter life was a big drear NOTHING to dream for, NOTHING to work for. I helped her find a first time buyer project and they were outraged at what had happened to her, she was able to buy a house that was returned for some reason, because she had done every single thing they had told her to do, and the foreclosures and returns were not in the line up of regular homes.

BUT, we ALL have to realize, for every program there has been for helping the poor or working poor to have their own homes, or better rented housing, there have been thousands of scammers, politicians and their hidden hedge funds and friends, who bought up property at low prices and sold them back at outrageous prices with interest (more than likely purchased from mortgage companies, or banks ALSO owned by friends of politicians) raising the housing price and rental costs for everyone.

WHEN WE GIVE, we have to have oversight to make SURE the taxpayers and poor are not getting defrauded and overcharged. WE must never forget that higher property values mean higher taxes, and MORE money for politicians to pay themselves and their palsies.

RESPONSIBILITY

Everyone in a family has responsibility. Everyone in a Democratic Republic such as America has responsibility.

Children need to learn as early as possible to honor their own responsibility.

This is a workbook for classes that are taught. YOU can become a trainer and bring YOUR local neighborhood together to live happily ever after. THE MYTH OF "THEY" IN AMERICA

Many people, especially politicians, live on a grand scale selling the ignorant the idea that someone else is to blame for their conditions. We, as a nation have seen the bad outcome of a strange idea that the very rich should have jobs paid for by the middle working class, to give food, housing, clothing and medical care to the VERY poor who work for the very rich. That idea made no sense from the outset. It ended up in the nine year depression started by the idea that if we moved SEVENTY THOUSAND of our factories to other countries that allow slavery and child slavery, and did away with import taxes and fees, we could sell the same packages with food, and other items inside that were packaged and processed by people so poor the most poverty stricken homeless in America can not even conceive of that level of demeaning poverty. People with NO bathrooms in the often outdoor factories under shed covers only, also have NO where to bathe, sleep, or wash their clothing or dishes except the irrigation canals. THEN the slaves out in the fields, living in the same conditions turn on the sprinklers and spray that water from the filthy canals on the food they export for FREE to America.

The poorest person in America, even a homeless with a pack of cigarettes, and a beer and a sandwich from the homeless catering vans has the requisite $15 of assets to be in the top ten percent of the richest people on earth. China, with more than a third of the world's population has technology, and good jobs, live in cramped apartments and go home to small farms the government has managed so far to salvage from big factory farms for a vacation now and then to see their families.

Russia and India are both attempting to figure it out, They have extremely rich people and poor people we can not even imagine. Eating out of trash cans behind markets and restaurants is a luxury to orphans, unwanted thrown away children, seniors and disabled persons who think they have had a great meal when they find a cat or dog food can with some food left in the bottom or sides to make soup with over a small camp fire of wood and paper found in the same garbage dump they find the cans and left over food in trash bags from homes where people are so rich it is unimaginable.

People in Africa and many S. American countries live in such fear, and danger they will WALK hundreds, and thousands of miles to get to horrible slums and even worse jobs just to have a hope of living a few more days without either the government, or gangs murdering them.

Children in many of these countries walk to what used to be called "barefoot" schools because the children walked, without shoes, to have school under a tree (IF they were lucky). The $75 a year bags of education materials from the UN were all the ONE teacher got for the students of all grades, often a hundred or more in the class. Yet these children often made it into the top grades and testing to get into boarding schools that helped them become doctors, nurses, and other people who would come back and help their own country be better for the next generations of children.

American children and their families need to confront some issues and make sure their children get a top level education and utilize it to help build not just their own lives, but the lives of children in the next generations. This is discussed in depth in the book "BIG LIZ, LEADER OF THE GANG" about safe streets work in areas where we did Racial Tension and Gang Abatement. It is easy to whine, and blame, it is actually not so hard to reach in and get people in local areas to fix their own lives to better the hopes and chances of the children coming up behind them.

TEACH your children that each of us in America is RESPONSIBLE for the bad things going on. Even if you have to make a choice to save a few dollars, and /or live in the garage of a relative or friend, YOU can leave a bad neighborhood behind. Just be sure you do NOT take the problems with you.

All over the world people try to get to certain areas so they can live better, they bring their own attitudes, and their own children along and soon the new area is as bad as the old one.

It takes careful agreement and NO denial when moving to get to something better.

Even people who think when they win the lottery, or get a big inheritance ALL their problems will be resolved, are wrong. They bring their own ignorance and failure to deal positively with finances along with them.

Example: People win the lottery and run right out and buy a mansion, an expensive car, a lot of expensive name brand clothing and within a couple of short years realize they can NOT afford the upkeep on the mansion and grounds (today, in S. California it is $180 per half day for a bonded cleaning crew). The gardeners are even more. Water is being monitored and people are FINED for using too much water and/or electricity. That fancy car is now depreciated, and not worth half what they paid for it. IF it needs a simple oil change it is NOT $38 at the local fast oil change station, NOR do you know the workers who LIKE you since you always tip them an extra $5 for taking excellent care of your car, and telling you what it might need and how to get the dealer to admit it and take care of it for a reasonable price. THEN DMV send in the annual registration, more than some less expensive cars four or five years old COST, along with a notice it has to be smogged. The expensive parts cost thousands of dollars when the vehicle fails to smog, as it will because either someone has stolen the expensive parts, or they have worn out, being manufactured to last only a couple of years to guarantee you will have to spend MORE on that vehicle.

The insurance on both the mansion and vehicle are higher than your current mortgage per month.

People NEED to learn about and understand finance, and teach their children to deal with reality about finance.

NEED AND WANT

The FIRST principle of finance is the difference between NEED and WANT:

NEED is what the body needs to survive. Clean air, Clean water, healthy environment (no litter, no sewage, no pollution, no poisons in the food, safe medical care, safe foods) education enough to get a good job to afford what the culture where you live requires. Shelter, warm clothing, jobs so you can work.

WANT is things you may desire, but are NOT necessary to life. While you may not LIKE the jogging pants and sweat shirt, and all weather coat and boots you are wearing to keep you alive, you will NOT die if it is not trendy, or high fashion, or does not have some one else's name on it.

To have the things you NEED and some of those you WANT, it is necessary to take some responsibilities. Keep the air, water, and land clean for yourself and others. Work with others to clean up the problems and keep everyone educated to keep everything clean and healthy. Get the most of the education you have available to you, make it stretch, use it to grow.

It is YOUR responsibility to teach your children how to live to have their needs met, and to meet their wants without harming themselves or others.

One of the Mother's in a court mandated project I was teaching for a domestic violence program necessitated by the large numbers of two veteran families following Desert Storm a young woman told us this story about her four year old. The little girl had been taught to save a small percentage of all money she got, in a real bank account. One day she saw something on television and decided she had to have it. Her Mother said, it is too expensive and not worth the money. I will help you figure it out IF you want it, so you can earn it. The little girl visited her aunts, Grandmothers, and other relatives and some close neighbors telling them that she would do some work for them and what it was she wanted. She made a deal with her Mother and Father about how much of her savings she could use for the item. They helped her understand it is not a good thing to spend every penny in savings for things you want, you might NEED that money, so save it. She worked HARD for some of the friends and relatives and all of them said she does a wonderful job. She asked her Mother why some of the people asked her to do little jobs and gave her more money, and others were quite picky about the job being done right and only gave her the agreed on amount. Her Mother said, because some of them love you and want you to learn to make a realistic evaluation of your worth, and then to be honest in giving that amount back, and some of them love you and want you to know they just want to help you. Both kinds of people love you. She earned the money, and went to buy the item. She looked at it in the store, and thought, and then told her Mother, that she had come to the conclusion it was NOT worth all that hard work!

This is an important lesson to teach your children so they can live happily ever after. Sometimes they can have what they want, and should help if need be, to have what they need, and they need to learn how to work it all out.

One of our programs is about HOW TO VISIT a mall, or amusement park, or even go to a party that requires gifts.

Children are expected to do research on the amusement parks, and figure out what their focus is when they get there. They are required to earn at least half of the money for the field trip with their class, or with their family. EVERY child is expected to learn enough math to figure out what something costs, what the tax will be (along with WHY we pay taxes) and take enough money for what they want to purchase.

My Mother, when we turned 13 gave us a checking/savings account. Each six months she gave us the money she had budgeted for school clothing and entertainment. Its amazing how less one wants a nice little black dress when one has to wear clothes that are being outgrown, and the same shoes from the past six months for another six months. AND to figure out what did a thirteen year old need a little black dress for??? It looked so wonderful on the actress in her favorite movie!

As we grew into our later teens, we were allowed to charge some items, but we learned the hard way how much more retail credit can be, we not only had to pay the interest on the credit card payment until we paid off the item, we had to pay our MOTHER and could not charge anything else until we paid off that debt.

How much easier to learn that lesson at 15, for a dress or shoes on sale, than to learn it later for a car you cannot afford, the payments, or is a poor trade in by the time it is paid off. And to learn that what you think you NEED because you see it, is NOT so wonderful as you do without things you NEED while paying off that already discarded item.

Many parents learn this financial lesson while teaching it to their children.

CHILDREN DO NOT HAVE A RIGHT
TO EVERYTHING THEY WANT

In a research project for a high risk youth program run by a Psychiatrist for the State lock down programs, it was discovered that a bed, shelter from the weather, and as little and boring as either a cold or hot wheat cereal with canned milk would keep parents out of prison for neglect.

While that is very minimal parenting, and the program was for children who were coming out of juvenile criminal facilities with a leg bracelet GPS system and NEEDED to be reparented, for success in their own lives, it is necessary for both parents and children to understand that CHILDREN DO NOT HAVE A RIGHT TO EVERYTHING THEY WANT.

YOU ARE NOT AN ADULT......when.....

Most juvenile criminals get into trouble with the law when they somehow get the idea that they are grown up when they.......

We have exercises in our program in which juveniles must list what and why things make them an adult.

Then we break down their belief system.

Ants, worms, fish have sex. Having sex is NOT an adult activity.

"Adult" movies and "Adult" magazines are NOT adutt in an way. They are sold for one purpose only, for dirty old men to pretend something is in their life that is not even real, and for juvenile boys to pretend that same something is in their life ......one young man was hiding a magazine, he was creating an imaginary sexual life with a woman in a photograph in the old magazine. Our program found a current picture of the woman who in fact had posed for the picture decades before. He took one look at that nice little old lady and threw away his magazine and started to work on his own problems with being friends with, and maybe some day having a real relationship with a woman his own age.

Young girls often have sex with older men, with nice cars. We ask them why women their own age take a pass on these wonder guys. They get it. Because a woman with a brain sees the nice car, the no job, the drug and alcohol addictions, and realize a good time guy met in a bar is NOT going to be so much fun when they marry and have kids and he is still off, in the bars having fun instead of home building a family.

Cigarettes and other addictions. Alcohol, drugs are easy....they are NOT adult, but they do give an excuse to act without responsibility, or to forget reality rather than deal with it and move on.

We ask the youth to figure out just how many cigarettes, or drinks, or drugs it will take to get friends to like them, or pay the rent, or pass a test they did not study for, or to get caught up so they can leave special ed. It helps young people to realize adults are not telling them NO because they do not want them to have fun, they are telling them NO because they want them to sidestep MORE problems, expense and health and criminal issues.

THEN ASK: if children and teens want to be adults, how come they are not doing the things that really ARE adult. We have not had ONE addict or teen pregnant boy or girl who went out and got a job and paid the mortgage or rent for their parents! We did not find ONE who went out and got a job and paid the car payments, gas, or insurance so their parents could have less ADULT things to do.

We find that kids who want to be adult fail to clean the house, clean the yard, go down to the home improvement store or on YouTube and learn how to repair the house or car, and go find jobs to make those repairs. All of these are ADULT activities.

To keep your child free to "live happily ever after" it is necessary to train them to know the difference between NEED and WANT, and what is truly ADULT and what is truly childish and immature.

CRIME AND PUNISHMENT
NOT "URRRS MOM, MINE"

Human beings need to learn a lesson, it is a simple one my two year old got clearly. How did I know??? He said clearly to me "NOT Urrrrs MOM, MINE". He had heard his brother, me, and others say to him not to touch things because the items were not his, and the person said MINE. His little boy, LOUD voice could often be heard to say NOT urr's Mom, MINE. Yes, he learned what yours and mine meant and never the twain shall meet.

My sons are 49 and 50 and it was many many years before they forgave me for taking the money from their piggy banks to buy gas to get to the gas station and bank when my disability check was late. I ASKED them, explained to them, but even though they said yes, they meant NOT YOURS, OURS, because it came up over and over during their lives no matter that I paid the money back along with hundreds of thousands for private school so they did not have to go be beaten up by most of the kids for being white, and the rest for being brown, being Native American those gang and racial tension ridden days made it dangerous for them to go to public school. No matter I gave them each money for down payment on NEW trucks each when I got one of my lawsuit settlements from my insurance companies and the corporation that caused TSS.

I have worked with adult criminals, who when I asked them to participate in surveys or interviews admitted NO ONE had ever said NOT YOURS, MINE to them, not even as adults in courts. They were punished for touching, eating, using things belonging to other people, but never given the clear message, NOT YOURS, MINE, along with the message, Stealing is not OK. NEVER a message that my body is mine, not yours, do not touch it, including assaults, rapes, drive bys, armed robberies, and murder.

They learned to play "Cops and Robbers" early at home, and brought it along to school, as young as pre-pre-school. WE discussed in their rehabilitation program groups that when we stop playing cops and robbers, the cops have to stop either being police, or playing cops. In police/citizen mediation and discussion surveys and group interviews, the police often admitted they had no concept of their job, listed in the police administration classes I took in college as being to "apprehend and detain", NOTHING about being dirty harry type judges, jury and executioners, no matter if they had the wrong person, or it was a misdemeanor.

More on this subject later, but ALL citizens need to understand that police are humans, and as my Grandfather, a homicide detective explained to us, you have no idea what they are dealing with that day. The day you "just" rolled a stop sign, that officer may have just left the scene of a group of tiny pre-school kids, holding their little rope in their tiny hands run down by someone who "just" rolled a stop sign......you do NOT want to try and say I "just" anything. JUST be polite, give your information as requested, and say thank you for your service in a polite voice after you have signed and received your ticket. BECAUSE, said my wise Grandfather, you might "just" get a baton or bullet between your eyes. Is it right? Of course not, but reality is real.

Police also have to learn there is NO excuse for being dirty harry types, judge jury and executioner. That is NOT their job. CITIZENS have to realize that cops are only cops for a shift, then they too are citizens, and POLICE have to realize that citizens are the ones they protect. Many citizens are very seriously mentally ill and need facilities to help them, some cities have recently take the position that if the city will not help mentally ill people, the police will, new programs in which the police give people, especially homeless the choice of going to jail, or to a homeless evaluation program which has programs that actually HELP both homeless and mentally ill persons the crime rates are going down and conflict between police and citizens is going down rapidly.

Parents, friends, other relatives and churches NEED to push all our politicians to make sure all our cities have these programs and keep a strict oversight on them. Baxter Ward, a County Supervisor in Los Angeles forty years ago created a mentor program for every person in a facility to HELP them and to keep oversight on them, and liaison between the person and their family for maximum support. It was FREE, all volunteer run and manned. It is now a paid program that in my experience is NOT working, otherwise we would not have so many mentally ill, disabled, seniors and poor on the streets.

We can NOT just ignore the problems.

Families have to find help for their out of control children and youth. Families need to demand that schools provide help for finding safe facilities for children and teens with problems. Just forcing teachers and students to put up with be assaulted, raped, called names so the school district can get more money for these "special" students is NOT helping anyone.

The UNIONS need to put their power and money behind these issues. The current LAUSD strike and the Governor of the State, as well as the Mayor having to step in and give money, the District offering ALL their financials to the Union with the thought that if the Union can find an extra penny anywhere to meet demands, they are welcome to try; show that in fact we have to stop the rhetoric and get our communities, states, and country back on track before we lose what four hundred years of people have worked hard to correct and make work, from a vision of a few who convinced each other to put their lives and fortunes on the line to create a government OF the PEOPLE, BY the PEOPLE and FOR the PEOPLE. We were warned, stay united, or we would all fail. There is no blame, like a family in divorce, we are at a point to unite and resolve our issues, or lose. We need our children and teens to understand this, they are the ones who may lose their inheritance if we fail.

In Transactional Analysis, and books such as "I'm OK, You're OK" (cite) and Games People Play (cite) one learns that I am wonderful, created uniquely, and so are YOU. BUT, most people learn to play games which in the end make us all losers, and either hurt one another, or hurt others, or be hurt by others.

A PERSON DOES NOT HAVE A RIGHT TO BE STUPID

This is not about IQ, many of the most educated, and high IQ people in history and alive today are fully STUPID.

It is necessary to teach your child that they have no right to be stupid. The other night two girls with HUGE behinds crawled out the window of a vehicle on the freeway, and did some dance on top of the car which slowed on the freeway, and put every other driver on the freeway at risk.

These girls first of all should have stood on top of that vehicle and had their friend take smart phone pictures of them dancing. That would have stopped the entire antic. They could NOT possibly have had any idea of how HUGE their behinds were in those videos they posted. Only a STUPID person would have put the other drivers at risk. It does NOT take the brightest bulb in the batch to know that if one of them had fallen OFF the vehicle other vehicles would have swerved and more than likely attempted to stop and caused accidents in which innocent people would have been killed or maimed.

Every day we see people doing STUPID things that put others in danger. Most of the people who do STUPID things are those who for some reason think what they are doing is trendy, and will make others think they are up with the times and amazing. They are NOT, they are STUPID.

Most teachers, principals, probation officers, parole officers and judges see immediately where young people got the STUPID gene. As soon as most parents dealing with school, or justice programs open their mouth, it becomes VERY obvious why their child is STUPID, and in trouble for endangering others.

One young man was in Court, his Mother, dressed more for pole dancing than Court also was frowzy and had a big mouth, she made no effort to control even before the clerk called her son's case. The Judge asked each juvenile to tell him why they were in Court and why he should consider them for a special project that would give them a chance to create their own self support contract, keep it, and if they did, at age 25 have their entire record erased, BUT, if the juvenile failed to meet his or her own contract, the entire sentence maximum would be set, as an adult, NOT a juvenile.

This young man started to blather about the "P….uh co….uh officers" arresting him for being ill and missing a day of school He did not get through the sentence before the Judge interrupted and asked if he wanted to reconsider what the truth was. The Mother jumped up and began to scream and swear that "they" were all against her poor sick boy.

The Judge told her to sit down and be silent, or be removed from the court and jailed herself for contempt of Court, AND have ALL her parental rights terminated as it was obvious what the problem with this young man was.

The Judge sent the young man for two weeks briefing on the program in a very intense juvenile program and said when he returned he hoped he had a better perspective on his life. In fact, the young man had not gone to school, and was in a store stealing things, passing the items over the security screen machine to others outside who ran away with the items. Unfortunately for this young man, the store security grabbed on to him, and a woman waiting at the cashier said, "this is your unlucky day" and asked the manager to call the police. The woman was one of the Court liaison workers for the probation department. She knew he was on probation and that he was ordered NOT to miss a day of school without being in the hospital or he would be remanded and all his cases would be heard together as an adult, his antics no longer considered juvenile.

STUPID

Parents often keep their children out of school to babysit so the parents can go out with friends, or shopping, or other selfish reasons that get their children into the Family Court system.

STUPID.

Parents are often evicted for not paying the rent. They are on welfare, get taxpayer funded housing, and only have to pay a small amount, but have never learned that when you get your check, pay for housing, utilities, vehicle to get to work or school, and care for the children, food, and NOT go out buying drugs, alcohol, clothing, or get nails or hair done or go clubbing BEFORE paying what the money is there for, to TAKE care of the children.

STUPID

NO ONE HAS A RIGHT TO BE STUPID and harm others, or cost others their lives, or property.

A major part of living happily ever after is learning not to be stupid. EXCELLENCE:

Parents need to teach their children to BE Excellent, by being Excellent themselves.

People who are excellent clean their homes and vehicles. DO not eat, or allow children to eat in the car. It takes several days or even weeks for over fed Americans to starve to death, Even if the whole family has to sit outside on the curb at the gas station every 250 miles while the car is gassed up, there is NO excuse to have a car filled with spilled drinks, spoiling food, and old food wrappers, as well as cans and bottle.

Neither you, nor your children are going to die of dehydration from not drinking in the vehicles.

There is NO reason for you or your children to wander around the house eating and drinking and leaving food wrappers, bottles and cans all around the house.

One of the most prestigious weight loss plans trains the members that one of the best ways to LOSE weight is to CHOOSE a formal place to eat, and eat in that place. To drink a glass of water BEFORE eating. Excellent parenting means teaching your children to eat nutritious food in appropriate amounts.

DO NOT LITTER your house, or street. It not only is a $1500 find in most cities to throw trash from a vehicle, it is NOT excellent. If you have the strength and a bag to put things into your vehicle, you have strength and a bag to put the wrappers and dirty diapers in and put them in your trash cans when you get home, or to a store or gas station which both have trash cans.

Our programs took gangsters on field trips to beautiful neighborhoods, with crowded small homes, and high risk, small apartment condo complexes. We pointed out, NO graffiti, NO gum, NO dirty diapers, NO trash. We said, if your home area is YOUR TURF, why is it so filthy. WE asked them, do you think Cheney lives in filthy nasty neighborhood like yours? He was in our view a bigger gangster than any of them.

LIVE IN EXCELLENCE. Shooting little old ladies and kids caught in the cross fire of cowardly drive bys, or running down anyone courageous enough to attempt to get to the other side if the street because one is too stupid to know that RACE CAR drivers are professionals who drive on tracks, or closed road tracks in professional race cars that are super well kept up, changing tires more than once in small, short 500 mile races….and YOU are just a stupe in a street junk is NOT excellent.

Ambushing police who are not expecting it is NOT manly, it is STUPID and cowardly. The big gangsters when these things happen have been known to throw a body out near the driveway of the police station with a NOTE on the chest saying what crime the STUPE has done because REAL gangsters know if you kill or shoot police, they close down all crime and real gangsters, like any other business person, do NOT like to have their business out of business, especially because of some stupe that is too stupid to be allowed in real gangs. It is NOT EXCELLENT.

Being an excellent parent means to help your child be excellent everywhere, in all things.

Part of being excellent is KNOWING the law and the history behind it. There are Americans who spend their time demanding Revolution, we HAD our revolution. People need to KNOW that socialism, capitalism, and communism are POLICIES of finance, the main base of all three is that a few have all the money and power, the rest of the people are serfs. The only difference between these POLICIES and a parliament based on a despot, or monarch is that the PEOPLE do not have any rights.

The history of American Democratic Republic has given the PEOPLE the right and the way to get civil rights, land rights, FOR the PEOPLE, not just a few. It was Hamilton who brought in the banks NO ONE wanted. The opera is great, the history flawed. Hamilton was an orphan, or possibly a sold off child to pay debts for his parents who grew up NEEDING power and money. He had NO idea of what he was destroying when he helped those greedy bankers and britishtribe supporters back into America.

A good parent needs to make sure their children know what is what and how to get change.

Women got the right to vote, and to be more than chattel to their husbands and fathers.

Native Americans got their vote and the right to be more than just the leftovers of a huge genocide by people who had recently discovered guns and canons and came with mercenary armies to commit genocide, make slaves of the men and boys, and sex traffick the women and girls, and murder the elderly, the children, and disabled. These habits are the same as they are described in the Bible itself for thousands of years. The American Founders, while some were very selfish and wanted those rights for themselves against the king of britishtribe land, did NOT want them for ALL Americans, including the Native Americans.

But flawed as it is, America has the RIGHT to make changes. Our current system of two parties of arguing over paid Congress who do NOTHING is NOT helping that happen. Our children, and we, need to study the CONSTITUTION and THE Manual of the

United States Government and realize that there is more than rights for criminals to wave the fifth amendment, and to use technicalities to get away with crime. The CONSTITUTION and government are SUPPOSED to protect and serve the PEOPLE. IF not, the Declaration of Independence tells us simply, to replace it. BUT we are the ones who continue to vote in the same over paid politicians that our Founders would NOT have wanted in power.

Voters have put in term limits, and are considering election reforms such as other countries have. MANY countries only allow a person to sign up or be nominated a few short weeks before an election for ANY position, and they can NOT campaign until after their paperwork is complete. What a relief, no more four year campaigns.

Every parent needs to buy a globe, and some books and video about the universe, space and how our earth and America fit into that universe. Every parent needs to buy maps and make sure their child knows every continent and every nation and at least every State of the United States and where it is before their child goes to kindergarten. Having taught at two of the most prestigious and expensive private pre schools and kindergartens, it is REQUIRED for all the students.

Along those lines, parents NEED to make sure their child does NOT get rejected by preschool, or fail pre school. Children need to know the difference between public and private. They need to know to NOT TOUCH ANYTHING THAT IS NOT THEIRS. Graffiti in other countries, where there is no freedom of speech may be a needed form of communication. In America it just costs the taxpayers more money. Children need to know if the parents own, or rent a home, they are paying to clean up that mess. When children or teens steal street signs, or freeway signs, they are raising the taxes for everyone.

SOLIDARITY

Like the word INDIGENOUS, this word is NOT what people think it is. The real first peoples of ANY land deserve to be at minimum called First People. Indigenous is a term that demeans the people by creating an academic ruse that they are respected, when in fact it means the bunny people, waiting for the amazing "civilized " to come along and steal their lands, put them to "work" and take away their assets, way of life, culture, and give them that amazing right to "debt" if they want to try and build any of their loss back to a livable lifestyle. READ the book Hawaii, by Michner. He says, they came to lighten the load of the heathens, they lightened it all right, they not only took the kitchen sink, but the buildings and land it was attached to.

Hawaii is great example: the people surfed, fished, had their herds and planted among the wild plants to keep a balance with nature. They had what we call scientists, and architects who told people where and how to build their homes so they would not be swamped in storms, or blown away in harsh winds. Now they have to pay code enforcement for permits to build on their own lands, their customs are called superstitions, while rich white people, at huge expense pay "feung shui" experts to tell them how to set up their homes and yards. AND only rich white people can afford to surf, fish, or use their boats on the coastlines.

In countries such as France in the story Tale of Two Cities, the word solidarity means something. In America it means groups against each other even after we were warned that to be divided would make America FAIL. Sixth graders learn that the clique girls and the bullying jocks make everyone else fight so no one realizes they are the ones causing all the problems. It is sad that this is what solidarity means to me. Instead of sitting down on the freeway, in your car, and getting everyone else to do the same to get rid of mandatory insurance that does NOT pay the innocent drivers, and keep the taxpayers from paying the health bills for those horribly maimed…….we say solidarity and nothing gets done. We need to teach our children to stand up for our rights, not to call each other names, march in opposition and nothing changes while we go home and say I did MY part.

I was really disappointed in the Pink Pussy Hat groupings. NOTHING happened. I had hoped that they would become annual, and semi annual local events DOING something for women, both locally and globally. IF every woman in the first event had just donated

$10 and then the next year donated another $10 for herself and as much as she felt she could afford for women around the world, Planned Parenthood would have an ongoing endowment started to provide FREE services world wide for ALL women, no more begging Congress or States to give a pittance.

WOMEN with Pink Pussy Hats could have created shirts demanding that sex trafficking be STOPPED, and laws be made that were enforced. MEN and BOYS would have to get it, and WOMEN AND GIRLS would be taught, if that man is so great, why don't women his own age want him…….oh, my Dad taught us, ….because the older women see that he has no job, no car, no nothing, and thinks he is still 18 and never is going to grow up.

One thing you have to say about ME TOO is that boys and men are now as afraid of women as they used to be of them.

Make sure your children learn that relationships are personal, and need to be equal, otherwise it is NOT a relationship, it is just some weird type of using of one or both parties that ends up making them both broken and their children broken as well. Modeling this is good start.

TOLERANCE

MAKE sure your children and YOU know the difference between the right to NOT LIKE anyone you want to dislike, and bothering in any way people you do not like. YOU do NOT have the RIGHT to "tolerate" anyone. What they have a right to is that YOU do not bother them in any way. Keep your mouth shut, your hands off them, and do not bother any of their business, or property rights.

People continue to believe that "tolerance" and "diversity" are gifts the bad guys "give" to everyone. THIS IS AMERICA. THE CONSTITUTION guarantees that every one has equal rights to live in freedom, with justice, and to pursue happiness in their own way as long as it does not harm other people.

An important part of being a good citizen or guest in America is to know what this means.

It means obey the law. OR CHANGE IT.

In most countries laws are created by an elite to favor THEM, there are many laws presently in America that fit that definition, but we have the tools to change those laws. Most of us do not even know they are being broken because they are too busy being the riff raff, the rabble being roused by the divisive people who want to make sure the "PEOPLE" are so busy hating and fighting they do not realize what is REALLY going on.

RELIGIOUS FREEDOM

The exact wording of the CONSTITUTION is that every person is guaranteed freedom to worship, or NOT as they want to. In support journal articles and newspaper articles it was plain that the FOUNDERS were tired, tired, tired of religious wars. They were not going to have any more of it.

Bob Dylan wrote a song "With God on OUR Side' which told us clearly that all the bad things people do in the name of GOD are NOT about GOD, but about greedy, lying, selfish people using God and religion to make their bad acts OK.

NO ONE has the RIGHT to put down another religion in America. BUT, the wording of the CONSTITUTION says the STATE can NEVER make one religion or another over other religions. The meaning, in context with the feelings of the Founders, most of whom had been forced at some time to pay for, if not be involved in "religious" wars, is that the Constitution and the GOVERNMENT are NOT to be used for dividing the people.

Please make sure your children are raised to understand being one of the mob, with pitchfork, and torch chasing Frankenstein's monster, and pounding in the door or burning his home is NOT what America is about, EVER. WE have not set a good example in the genocide of the original people, who DID in fact have their own immigration laws, and a system of laws that Franklin studied that encompassed more than 800 Native Nations who had lived together in peace for centuries keeping a balance with nature by keeping the herds, waters, and fowl protected from "greedy" who thought it was OK to just strip the lands to make money and strip the forests, and kill anything that moved or breathed to make money selling it to the euro environmentally stupid who had over populated and stripped their own lands but had managed to invent guns so came a marauding.

We have not, as a nation set a good example going about, against the CONSTITUTION to support the empire building of other nations. The soldiers from Korea, Vietnam, Laos and Cambodia still are wondering if we thought maybe those people in their rice fields, or banana forests (they knew banana plants have to grow with other plants, or they get diseased and die, harming the land right along with the death of the plants (it is in a documentary on all the HUGE banana nations now bare, shown by satellite trying desperately to raise a hybrid plantain to salvage their factory farms)were going to get in their little reed boats, and throw rice balls at us. After the war got to going, and both sides seemed to be buying a lot of the same weapons, the soldiers began to realize the black market was stealing their weapons and selling them to those fighting them. AND they wondered, why were Blacks, Native Americans and poor whites killing poor rice farmers in their own lands for some rich guys to sell weapons, and steal the lands. Those soldiers were called anti-war traitors. MASH, the book and the movie were NOT popular because they made people think, and let them know what was really going on. Make sure your children know that movies and television shows are one thing, reality is another. We have three million "honored" veterans who live in prisons, and homeless in the streets because the bureaucrats who run the "denial paper stations and courts" are taking all the money needed to help the veterans. The latest VA hospital, recently finished in months, was not scheduled to be finished for years, at a huge over run on the bid. It came in fast, and for a lower price.

Most veterans in prison are there because of untreated PTSD. As one of the VA doctors said to his staff, every one of those veterans was physically, emotionally, and mentally fit enough to send to give their life for America. Treat them with respect, if they are now broken, it is in service of America, and they deserve the best of care and treatment.

WE all have hard work to do to get to "happily ever after", but much of it can be joyful work and bring us all together to grow our principles, and inspire other countries to do the same.

Children are the easiest. Research has shown that NO child is born hating, or with mean thoughts, or actions. ALL bad behavior is learned. ALL bad behavior can be changed. NOT all parents, or teachers, or psychologists are fit to do this task. Today there is new evidence from the VA that much of PTSD and other behavior problems can be traced by tests to neurological damage. Even athletes are being given better safety gear and rules due to neurological damage and its effect on behavior and quality of life. BUT, even severely brain injured persons can be in programs that help them adjust to their disability and be better citizens.

Be careful what you say in front of children.

Stand up for what is right if it is safe.

In the book "Big Liz, the Leader of the Gang", I went into gang territory and asked the real gangsters for their help to make their neighborhoods better for the kids coming up behind them. They were awesomely agreeable and did help.

The following is about the series of workshops and books "LIVE HAPPILY EVER AFTER" and the author.

This book is a challenge, a hope, a push to make yourself, your family and your city, county, state and our nation, along with the world a better place for everyone, and everything It is a challenge to YOU to find what you personally NEED and want to "live happily ever after..." and to create the changes needed to make that a reality. It is a challenge to you to find out what your family, job, block, or apartment floor need to "live happily ever after..." and to create the changes needed to make that a reality.

WARNING: this book is written by retired old persons, with concussions and brain injuries thanks to those who injure others without concern. This is NOT an APA book written for grammar critics. Do not bother to write and criticize, we do NOT read or consider mean people's thoughts on our use of commas, semi colons, or colons or language use. Go bother the mean people, the criminals, drunk drivers, the corporate leaders and lawyers, and politicians who allow horrible injury to others without care, or consequence.

Abraham Lincoln is alleged to have said, "YOU will be as happy as you make up your mind to be". It is a key to the gateway of being happy. Eleanor Roosevelt is alleged to have said it is up to each of us to choose to let the opinions and criticism of others harm us, or NOT. Joyce Meyer invented the excuse bag, and the God bag. She took real handbags, and in one put the excuses to not live happily ever after, and in the other put those excuses, one by one, handing them over to God as each person used those burdens as building blocks, or stepping stones, rather than roadblocks, to let them find a way to help themselves and others avoid the pitfalls, and/or to overcome the injury and inner pain of real life injuries.

Most of our work is done with veterans, first responders, and high risk youth and their families. Most of them, if not all, have excuse bags overflowing, yet most of them learn to admit, address and give their excuses to the God bag. In some retreats for women veterans, and single parent mothers sent to us in mandatory Court ordered programs to earm custody of their children back, we have used a God gift box, in which as the retreat proceeds, the group members give up their excuses and burdens and give them to God to handle.

Our groups and seminars ALL start with an introduction, whether on a name tag, or out loud in a breakaway group, EVERYONE is asked to say this simple phrase. "My name is___, I am wonderful because our Creator made me," We ask each participant to stand up in front of the group, or in the talking circle, read this sentence and tell us something wonderful and unique about themselves.

As discussed below, we do NOT require that anyone believe in our idea of a Creator, or any one religious practice or belief. We do however discuss that like breath, it does not matter, over the centuries and centuries of humans on this earth, without breath, we can NOT live, and our position is that without a faith in something (even if, like Bill Maher, it is a faith that there IS no God) we each NEED some kind of belief to uphold us when times are great, to thank that entity, or when times get hard, to lean upon. Even the staunchest of atheists needs a community of like believers to trust and lean on when the time comes, and to celebrate with when the sun comes up and they are still breathing. Most old old old people (like us) know. It is a gift to be grateful for to have one more day. NO MATTER WHAT.

PERSONAL STORY

This story is in small part the reason for writing this book: There are many other parts in other books.

One day, driving in a borrowed vehicle, mine had been totally destroyed by two drunks racing, and they said it was MY fault, the one who stayed at the scene, rather than hit and run as his palsy did, had my same insurance company. The company said, we just found a great way for us to not have to pay anyone, we will find you both equally at fault, you have to pay your own damages. It also led to almost six years before an MRI was paid

for by Social Security (I had retired by then and had full retirement Social Security that paid for any condition, and did NOT argue that auto insurance, either mine, or the drunks should pay for care). It was found the reason my legs were not able to move was they had bone injuries, combined with arthritis in the untreated conditions, and I needed a hip replacement. Due to the long years of not being treated my back and other leg, and all the muscles and soft tissue were injured enough to keep me still working on crutches and braces to learn to walk again, almost eight years later. Kind of hard for a horse trainer and equine therapist. I have not given up.

My sister Eva, and my sister (in law) Judith had died of cancer, leaving their teen and college age children without mothers, as well as two broken men to raise children alone. My Mom and Dad had passed away, from old age, expected, both were in hospice care, but still, a hard blow.

AND having found out the research levels of radiation that had saved my life from deadly stage four, level four cancer had just been diagnosed as the cause of internal bleeding.

The doctors sadly said, we told you when you volunteered for the research that we "might" be able to give you an extra two years, and we have more than done that, but we have no treatment for the radiation caused internal bleeding. I prayed for an answer. A friend with breast cancer, with implants that kept being rejected and having surgery after surgery told me she had been referred to a wonderful Osteopath and nutritionist who had helped her begin to heal. I went, saying to myself, I do not care if he says eat pebbles or marbles, I will do it and heal. He said eat overcooked rice, a zucchini and green been parsley soup put through the blender, and steamed fish to help the radiation burned intestines heal. A big treat, once in awhile meal was overcooked oatmeal and a few organic blueberries to make sure no chemicals were eaten on either the berries or the oats. Ten months into this hard to keep program, I asked him if I could eat a piece of home made angel cake, and some whipped cream and a strawberry or two for my birthday. He was surprised that I was still on the nutrition program, and that much still keeping to the

program. I was sent for a colonoscopy. I had healed. I did not have to return for ten years for a follow up. Thank God, but that too had been a huge stress in many different ways.

AND we were looking for a new stable for our equine therapy program because a jerk with a flowers in his hair and his old hippie friends had taken over the ranch we had rented part of.........I was truly upset.

I had spent over $35,000 of my own money, borrowed and paid back $30,000 from friends and family, and had a student debt of $73,000 to earn a PhD. IF I had stayed at Cal Tech/La Verne where I started while employed in a science project I would have had less or no student debt, and gotten my degree. BUT I had what turned out to be cancer and was bedridden, so went to online. What a mistake. The promised ADA Brain damaged support mentor was not there, and the final thousands of dollars to get a writer and editor were NOT covered as they had promised and would have been at Cal Tech/La Verne where I started my work in Reassessing and Restructuring Public Agencies. I had completed ALL my work, with a 3.74 average, even with APA deductions on each paper, and even without the promised statistics ADA aide. LUCKILY the drunks racing hit me, and put me worse disabled and the loans were charged off due to the injuries ending my work. Except for almost ten thousand in loans from a bank

I had not been told were NOT on my Federal Student loan program. A PhD without the final paper is useless.

Depressed.

I was driving along, and said, to our Creator (being Native American) I need a sign.

Somewhat like the movie Bruce Almighty, I turned the corner, and there, leaned against a trashcan, was a BEAUTIFUL sign. I could see the people had had a big party, as many trash cans were filled with pink tablecloths, and surrounded by pink tablecloths tied around the left overs and big black trash bags filled with party things. I knew the lady who owned the house briefly. I stopped and stared at the sign.

One day I had seen her Christmas decorations blowing off the fences and shrubs and down the street. I stopped to help her get them back. We stood on the truck bed of my four wheeler to put them back more securely.

One day I had seen her trying to get oranges off her trees, and again had stopped to help, the kids and we jumped up in the truck bed and got the oranges. I knew she would not mind my taking that sign on the street outside her trashcans.

I thought, unlike Bruce, I am going to heed this sign and took it up to my stable. The sign read..........

.....happily ever after......

I thought this is JUST what I need.

I put the sign up and everyone who saw it, wanted one. We told the kids and the veterans, and the first responders and their families, as well as our volunteers to make their own posters, signs, and shirts with these words on them. We began to teach classes in probation and lock downs, in veteran groups, to single Mothers. Make your own poster, sign and/or shirt as the groups talked about their dreams, and their disappointments and began their own workbooks on rebuilding, or building a life in which they could live "happily ever after…..".

We found another stable, and what a nightmare. We ended up suing the city over an overzeaolous and/or corrupt animal control officer and moved to another COUNTY. Long story, it is in our book about equine therapy.

In the meantime one of our Board members died of MS. Our Director finally got her MRI from being assaulted by a student who should NOT have been in a public school, and it turned out to be a blessing, they found newly beginning spinal cord cancer and she had two surgeries, added to the surgeries she needed after being assaulted by the student.

The animal control Gestapo (as our lawyer called her when filing papers)was calling her in the intensive care unit, saying she BETTER get out and deal with her or go to jail. She could NOT reach me, because, as life will sometimes do, my cell carrier was putting in a new system and merging with another larger company and we could NOT use our cell phones. I did NOT use a home phone, I was always with the horses or doing a free seminar for high risk youth, veterans, and first responders and their families. We were paying $12,000 a month for a rented stable, and the staff to live in the house and care for the horses. One of them was a professional rodeo champion and owned her own horses, and her friend had helped her with her horses for years. Both the Director and I raised our own funds, and used our own disability and retirement payments to do this work. I closed my teachers retirement account to pay for the move and deposits to get the horses into the sanctuary and safe, after the events mentioned below. I have paid each month to keep the horses safe, letting the veteran run stable utilize them for their veteran and youth programs. These were all trained therapy horses in different levels of training and capabilities. This is discussed in another book.

We found a new stable, and moved every thing we had. Not more than two or three hours after unloading, a fast moving forest fire changed direction due to winds, and in less than 30 minutes the fire passed so rapidly every thing was burned, the steel bars warped, some of the welds melting out. The aluminum bars and covers burned, bent, along with the sheds, tack, feed, and office and garden items. ALL gone. Again, luckily, the woman driving the big stock trailers to bring the horses had called to say she had to get on a plane, family emergency in another state and did not move them that day. SO, the horses ALL were safe in their old stable, just all together, we had taken all the pens, arenas, and round corrals. The small animals had been taken by car and truck to another therapy program, so they too were safe. Of course the over zealous Gestapo woman wrote us up for the horses being in a huge lot, rather than stalls as well.

The sign had been in my friend's car, and left off at my home. There it was, each day,

….happily ever after….. By then two more Board members had had

severe health issues and moved away to family members states for care and love.

The State had investigated the by then long ago vehicle accident, so slowly that their report, that said the TWO racing drunks who hit me had been going over 80 mph when they hit my big fourwheeler, turning it to junk did not come until the statute of limitations had gone, so claimed the insurance company. I had to keep paying off the contract, since the insurance company had found both parties equally guilty…….
and the Statute of Limitations had run to sue the company So much for being there! Luckily I only owed a few more months on the contract. The credit union was very surprised and happy that I did just pay off the contract on a totaled vehicle.

In the meantime I had received a recall notice on the truck, which said it would take off on its own when the brake was released. I called and said, well, it's a little late, the truck is totaled and the guys who hit me said the truck had jumped out at them, and months before I had gotten a ticket for the truck taking off across a six lane roadway FAST when I released the brake, right in front of a cop with a radar gun.

I had to pay for traffic school, and the traffic school teacher had been super sick with a long lasting flu which I was fortunate to get. They said NO problem, we are going to take care of it, sent an email application, and two years later a snotty lawyer said, OH, you should not have believed us, you should have filed a lawsuit. Even though they were my favorite vehicle, I will never buy a Toyota again.

So, I needed my sign.

…..."happily ever after".

I was, for a little while since putting the horses in a safe ranch, loaned to another therapy program to reduce my costs to keep them alive, sitting on the couch, with Joyce and Joel, and other inspirational speakers of many religions looping over and over on my cable recordings. And going to my own church at least twice a week. One day my older son said "you know Mom, you have to eat". I said "I am doing the best I can". We both laughed. I looked at my sign and went off to help care for our Director who had just gotten out of hospital. I had to take two busses and walk on crutches and braces to get up to her house, but she was not doing so well, even with an everyday nurse dropping by.

We said, … **"happily ever after"** and decided to hang on and reorganize and

get restarted. The project "48 Acres" described below, was left hanging in a day when the Governor, to make himself look great for reducing costs to the state, canceled and closed the State Redevelopment Agency that had ASKED us to donate our time and experience as a team to design and develop the project expected to provide services to more than 70,000 returning Afghan and Iraq veterans and their families. They were kind enough to tell our group of retired old persons that we could buy the land donated by the city and provide the building and services ourselves. More on that below, and in another book. WE began to look for ways to facilitate for our expected clients to live "happily ever after…" and help each other.

WE ourselves, over the decades had to stop and make up our minds to live "happily ever after", and we want to share our concept as we once again embark on our vision to build three tiered treatment and housing programs with and for veterans, first responders, and high risk youth and their families. SO, we decided to choose to live happily ever after, and share that with others. That is what this book is about. We encourage people to contact us and schedule town halls, or local area meetings to find out how to make your family, your block, your city, county, state and America live happily ever after..

OTHER BOOKS BY AUTHOR

Reassessing and Restructuring Public Agencies: What to do to save our Country

Carousel Horse-a teaching inclusive book about equine therapy

Spirit Horse II: Equine therapy manuals and workbooks

Could This Be Magic- a VERY short book about the time I spent with VAN HALEN

Dollars in the Streets-Lydia Caceres Edited by Author about first woman horse trainer at Belmont Park

Addicted to Dick –a healing book quasi Twelve Step for women with addiction to mean men

Addicted to Dick-2018 Edition Self help and training manual for women who allow men to torture, molest and kill their children

BOOKS TO BE RELEASED:

America CAN live happily ever after: first in series of Americans resolving all the issues

America CAN live happily ever after 2: Second in series of HOW to go out and BE equal, and to part of the OF the, BY the and FOR the People our Constitution guarantees us. If the school is not teaching your children, go down and read, do math, join a science project, do lunchtime Scouting for the kids, go sit in the hallways with your smart phone and take lovely action video for the parents of kids who do not behave. More. Many suggestions from parents, and how to fundraise.

Carousel Two: Equine therapy for veterans

Still Spinning: Equine therapy for women veterans

Legal Ethics: An Oxymoron???

Friend Bird: A children's book about loneliness and how to conquer it (adults will love it too)

Kids Anonymous and Kids Jr. quasi twelve step books for and by youth and teens

12 Steps Back from Betrayal from Brothers at Arms and 12 Steps Home two quasi twelve step books and work books created by author and veterans, and author's Father for Native American and other veterans

BIG LIZ: The Leader of the Gang Racial Tension and Gang Abatement work by author

PLEASE join the tee shirt contests by checking the web sites on the books and contacting the link provided. WE love children, teens and adults helping us to give our classes free, and spread the word of our work. ALL of our work is done through education projects by our high risk youth, veterans and first responders page NATIONAL HOMES FOR HEROES/SPIRIT HORSE II. We are just getting back to full work due to cancer of the two Directors and vehicle accidents and our stable burning down in a forest fire a couple of years ago. We promise to get more organized as we move along. 2019 is our first year of taking nominations and awarding a Keiry Equine Therapy Award. We will also need poster and tee shirt designs for that. See Carousel Horse and Spirit Horse II links to nominate a program.

God bless us, as Tiny Tim said, Every one.

The photographs in this book are by Tim G. Wiley or the author.

The photographs were chosen to help you help yourself and your children see all the wonder that is around us each day, but we are so busy trying to get some trendy thing, we fail to notice or be grateful for the beauty and gifts of nature around us.

Use the photographs to get your children interested in gardening, in volunteering at animal rescues or the pound to help raise funds for spay and neuter, to make sure they know that any abuse of an animal, for fighting, sports, or just not taking proper care of it is NOT OK. Many cultures believe GOD put us here to take care of nature and the animals for the next seven generations to enjoy. AND it is fun to see them, and help those who are helping the animals and nature be restored.

God bless us EVERY one. Including those who do not believe in God. I believe God knows our heart, and if people are kind and caring about nature and each other, that is more important than what religion they belong to or do not belong to.

Printed in the United States
By Bookmasters